PRACTISE TOGE…
SERI…

MENT…
ARITHMETIC

Activities, games and
helpful hints

Roger Hepworth

Illustrated by David Woodward

A Piccolo Original
Piccolo Books

[redacted]

Note to parents

Importance of mental arithmetic

In spite of the ever-increasing use of calculators, mental arithmetic and the ability to use it are still very important. The main reasons for this are:

1. In some circumstances, doing arithmetic in your head is still more efficient than using a calculator.

2. In order to use mental arithmetic effectively, children need to understand the structure of numbers and this in turn helps with their written maths.

3. It has been proved that people who can do mental arithmetic efficiently and confidently often use different methods from the ones they are taught to use on paper. It can be very helpful for children to have these differences demonstrated.

The activities in this book are designed to take these points into consideration, and they aim to offer interesting ways of learning number facts and to show how the structure of the number system can be used to simplify calculations so that they can be done in your head.

Level of difficulty

Children need to know their tables and number bonds to 20 reasonably well before attempting most of the activities in this book. (See Practise Together TABLES 1 & 2, also published in Piccolo, for further practice of tables if necessary.) It is advisable to do these activities in the correct order.

Calculators

Using a calculator is not discouraged, so let your child have one available while he or she is working through the book, although in certain activities there is clear guidance if it is best not to use a calculator. This is indicated with the symbol below. One of the book's aims is to help children to choose between using the calculator and using their own mental ability.

Mathematical words

Schools often introduce children to a correct mathematical vocabulary. We have included a glossary of some of these words in the back of the book, to help parents who may be less familiar with them.

Working through the book

These activities are meant to be enjoyed and when they stop being fun it is time for a rest and a change. So encourage the child to work in short bursts.

Your involvement and interest are very important and although the activities can be tackled by the child alone, we hope the book will provide opportunities for discussion between you.

The notes in boxes on most pages give guidance and hints to parents. In order to avoid using him/her and he/she, we have referred to the child as 'she' in these notes.

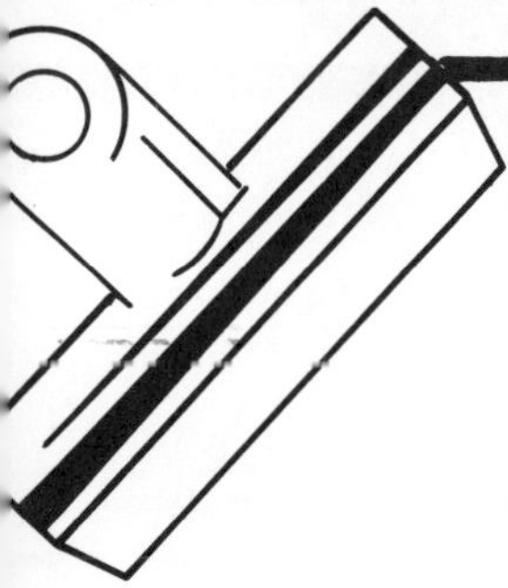

PATTERNS WITH TEN

Join the numbers which add up to ten, but don't use a calculator. Use different colours to draw the lines, or colour in the patterns you make. The first diagram has been started for you.

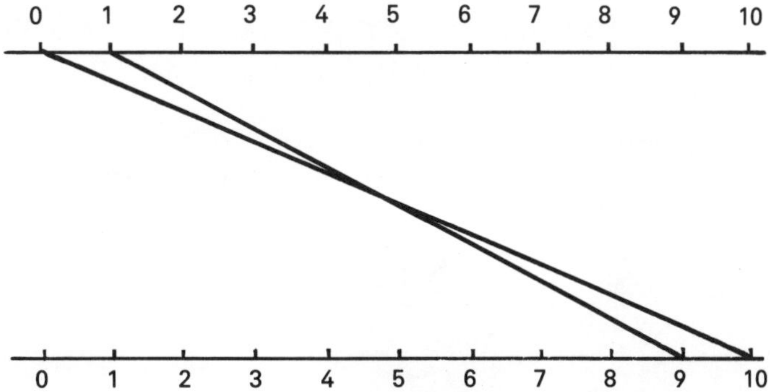

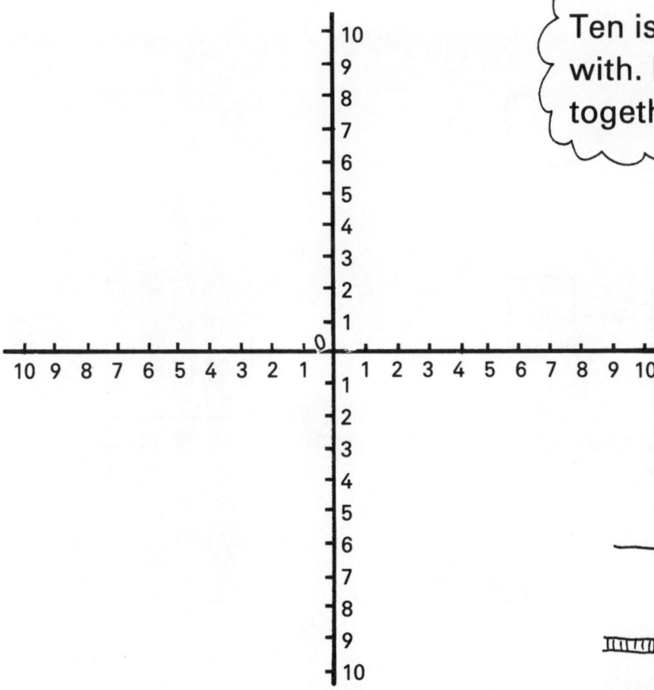

You will find that making sets of ten is an important short-cut in mental arithmetic, and crops up throughout this book.

MAKE TEN

You can think of any number as the sum of two other numbers.
e.g. Think of 6 as 4+2
Think of 9 as 7+2

You can use this idea to help you with addition.
e.g. Think of 8+6 as 8+ (2+4)

So now you can work it out in two stages.
8+2=10 and 10+4=14

Did you spot that the number to be added is split, so that the first part of the calculation adds up to a complete set of 10!

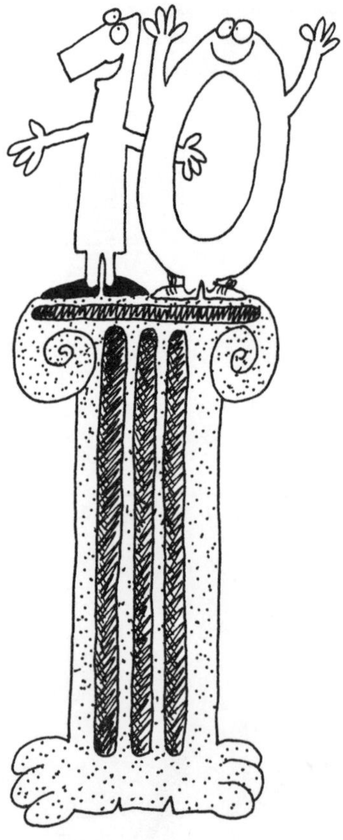

Try these examples yourself:

Think of 8+7 as 8+ (+5)

So 8 —+□→ 10 —+□→ □

Think of 9+3 as 9+ (+   )

So 9 —+□→ 10 —+□→ □

Think of 8+8 as 8+ (+   )

Think of 7+4 as 7+ (+   )

Think of 9+9 as 9+ (+   )

Now try these in your head:

7+7=	9+6=	9+4=
8+7=	7+6=	7+5=

You can also use this idea when you need to add units to numbers over 10.

e.g. Think of 15+7 as 15+ (5+2)
so: 15+5=20 and 20+2=22

Think of 37+6 as 37+ (3+3)
so: 37+3=40 and 40+3=43

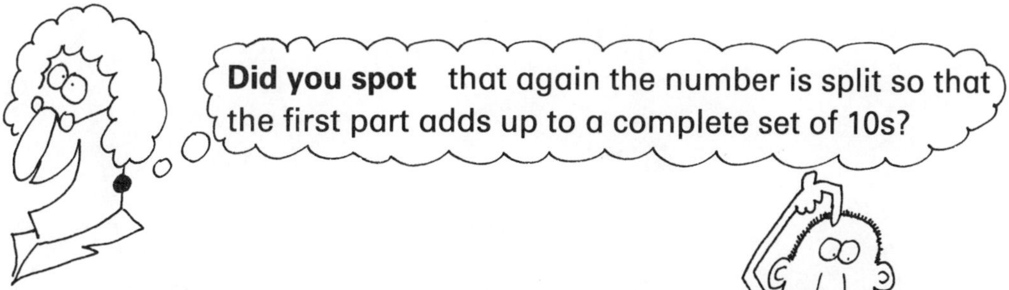

Now try these in your head:

19+3=	27+5=	15+6=
24+8=	37+8=	39+7=
43+9=	55+6=	54+6=
38+5=	48+4=	33+7=
44+9=	65+7=	51+9=

TWENTY UP

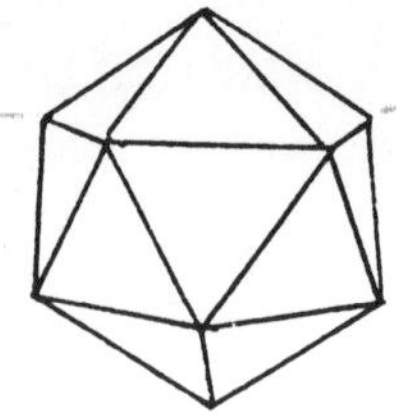

Trace this net onto card and then cut it out. Score all the lines, then bend along these lines and glue the net together using the tabs provided. Ask for help, if necessary.

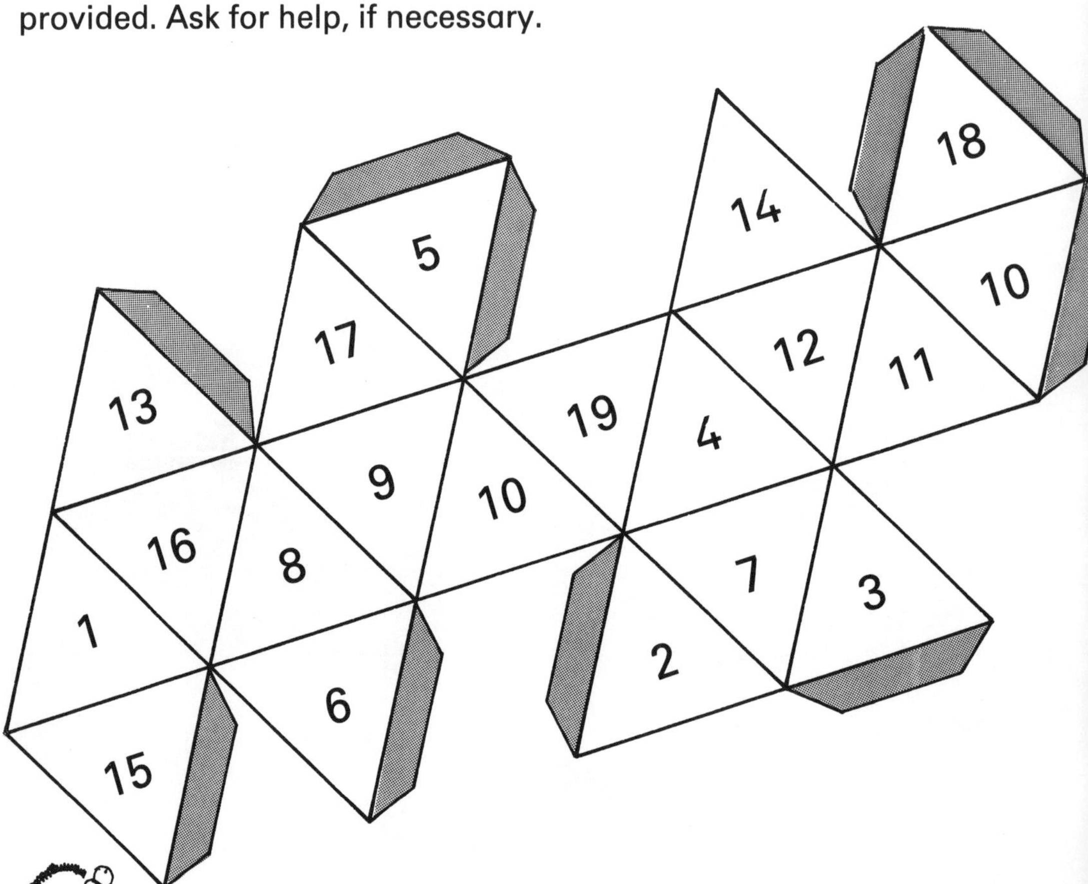

The solid shape you have made is called an Icosahedron and you can use it to astonish your friends!

Here is a chart of the pairs of numbers printed opposite each other on the Icosahedron. Add up these pairs of numbers. What do you notice?

	IS OPPOSITE		
1	→	19	1+19=
2	→	18	2+18=
3	→	17	3+17=
4	→	16	4+16=
5	→	15	5+15=
6	→	14	6+14=
7	→	13	7+13=
8	→	12	8+12=
9	→	11	9+11=
10	→	10	10+10=

If you can memorise these pairs of numbers, you'll be able to amaze your friends by telling them the number on the hidden face of the Icosahedron.

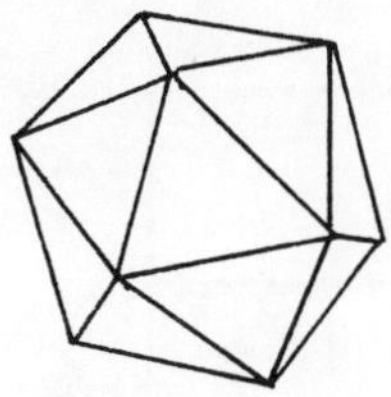

The aim of this activity is to help the child to learn her number bonds to 20. Younger children may need some help in constructing the Icosahedron.

BOXED IN

Can you fill in the missing numbers in these puzzles?

In each puzzle, add the pairs of numbers from left to right and then top to bottom, writing the answer beside or below.

When these new numbers are added together, they must equal the number in the 'corner' box. The first one has been filled in for you, as an example.

4	1	5
		+
3	5	8
7 + 6		13

9	4	
2	8	

5		7
	3	4

	6	
2		4
7		

	6	
4		
8	9	

	6	
6		
	11	21

SQUARE DANCE

Can you see that in Set A and Set B below, the same three numbers are repeated in each line? They are all connected and once you know one, you should be able to work out the others without calculating them.

Set A

9+2=11
2+9=11
11−2= 9
11−9= 2

Set B

8+5=13
5+8=13
13−5= 8
13−8= 5

Try this out to fill in these number squares.

40	−	9	=	31
−				+
31				9
=				=
9	+	31	=	40

63	−	8	=	55
8			=	63

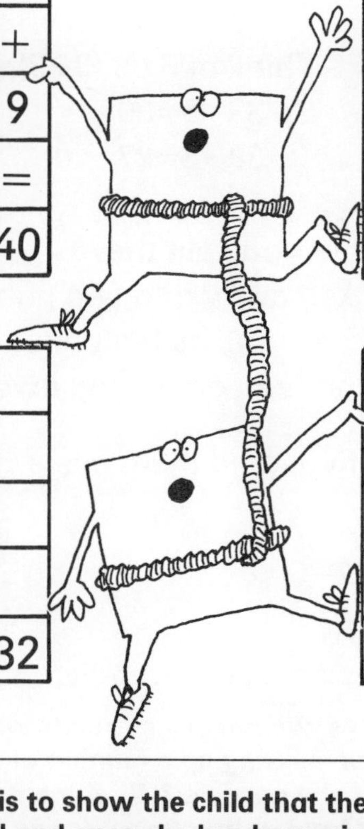

8	+	24	=	32

				23
				+
				17
				=
				40

The aim of this activity is to show the child that the numbers in calculations like these are connected and once she has been given one combination, she should be able to work out the others in her head.

TAKE IT AWAY

Try these two sets of calculations in your head. Which do you find harder to do?

	Set A	**Set B**
(a)	16−8	20−4
(b)	24−7	40−3
(c)	33−6	30−9

Most people find Set A more difficult.

Now look at this method which makes Set A as easy as Set B.

(a) 16−8

Think of 8 as (6+2), so now you can do the sum in two stages:
16−6=10 and 10−2=8

And (**b**) and (**c**) would be like this:

(b) 24−7

Think of 7 as (4+3)
So 24−4=20
20−3=17

(c) 33−6

Think of 6 as (3+3)
So 33−3=30
30−3=27

Did you spot that you split the number to be taken away into two numbers? One of these is the same as the units digit of the number you are taking away from.

Now try these and see if you find them easier.

23−8=	34−7=	13−9=
45−6=	22−5=	53−8=
35−8=	36−9=	43−6=

This exercise demonstrates two important points which you should explain clearly to the child: 1) That splitting up a number and subtracting each part separately does not affect the answer. 2) That mental methods of calculation often need to be different from written ones. Trying to do the subtraction in your head as you would do it on paper would be, in this case, more difficult.

ALL FOR NOUGHT

Find the difference between the pairs of numbers at the corners of the biggest square. Write the answer at the mid-point of each side. Keep doing this for each square until you reach the smallest one.

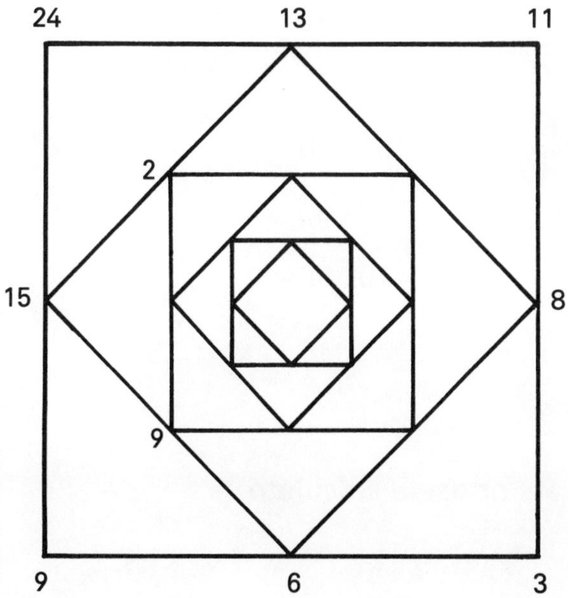

On the first square, some have already been done for you.

What do you notice about the number patterns?

Draw some more squares of your own and try different starting numbers.

ADD A TEN

How many of the following can you do in 3 minutes?

10+10=	10+20=	10+30=
20+10=	20+20=	20+30=
30+10=	30+20=	30+30=
40+10=	40+20=	40+30=
50+10=	50+20=	50+30=
60+10=	60+20=	60+30=
70+10=	70+20=	70+30=
80+10=	80+20=	
90+10=		

Ask someone to check your answers or use a calculator.

Did you spot that all the answers end in zero and that only the figure in the tens column changes in each calculation?

Use this hint to help you complete the following patterns quickly.

16+10=	23+10=	47+10=
16+20=	23+20=	47+20=
16+30=	23+30=	47+30=
16+40=	23+40=	47+40=
16+50=	23+50=	47+50=

There are more like this for you to try on the next page.

Try doing these examples in your head while a friend does them using a calculator. You should finish first!

22+10=	56+20=	43+20=
18+30=	31+40=	60+31=
20+19=	43+20=	29+70=
70+18=	64+30=	36+30=

What about *taking away* whole sets of 10?

e.g. 31−10=21 53−20=33

Did you spot that, again, only the tens digit of the figure you are taking away from changes?

Try these:

45−10=	98−40=	73−60=
48−30=	81−50=	39−20=
67−50=	41−40=	95−90=
80−40=	39−10=	52−30=
19−10=	46−30=	88−70=

By the end of this page, the child should realize that when whole sets of 10 are added or taken away, only the number in the tens column changes. She should also realize that there is no need to use a calculator here.

TENS

Here is the ten times table written out for you.

1×10=10	6×10= 60
2×10=20	7×10= 70
3×10=30	8×10= 80
4×10=40	9×10= 90
5×10=50	10×10=100

Did you spot that all the answers end in zero?

Use your calculator on the examples below to check if this always happens when a number is multiplied by ten.

97×10=	79×10=	84×10=
142×10=	342×10=	196×10=
869×10=	650×10=	100×10=

At the end of this page, check that the child has realized that any number multiplied by 10 will end in zero.

Now see if you can draw an arrow from each number in Set A to a number in Set B which is ten times bigger.

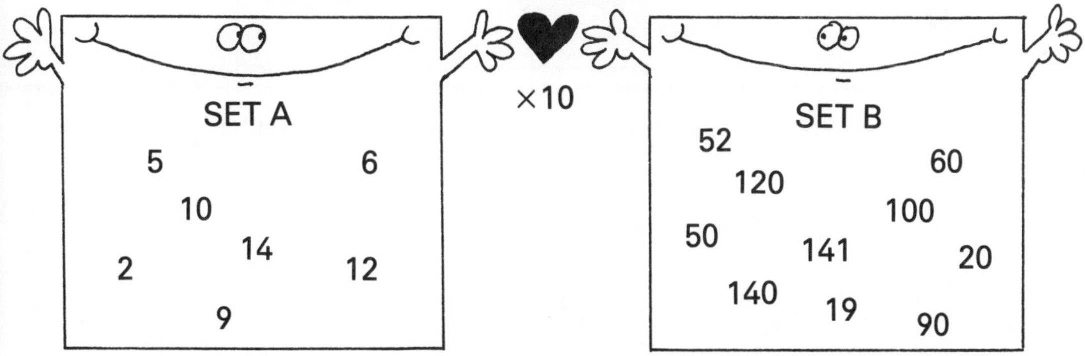

Using the numbers from Set B, fill in this chart:

Hundreds	Tens	Units	
		2	×10
	②	⓪	
		5	×10
	⑤	⓪	
		6	×10
	○	○	
		9	×10
	○	○	
	1	0	×10
○	○	○	
	1	2	×10
○	○	○	
	1	4	×10
○	○	○	

Never tell a child that to multiply by 10, you 'add a nought'. This is a trick which does not help real understanding and which only works in certain circumstances. If you were to 'add a nought' for 1.8×10, for example, it would give 1.80, which is wrong!

STEP DOWN

How quickly can you fill in the missing numbers on these table steps?

Here is an example for you:

3×1= 3
3×3= 9
3×9=27
3×7=21
3×1=3!

3×2= 6
3× =
3× =
3×4=
3× =6

7×1=
7× =
7× =
7× =21
7× =7

8×2=
8× =
8× =
8× =
8× =

This activity gives practice in the times tables and also demonstrates the digits pattern of each table. Encourage interested children to construct their own steps using different tables and different starting points, e.g. 6×3 or 7×4.

FOUR IN A ROW

Here is a game for two players. You will need 8 counters.

Take it in turns to choose a square on the board. Then choose two numbers, one from each column, A and B, which you think will produce the number in the square you have chosen when you multiply them together. If you are correct, place one of your counters on that square.

The winner is the first player to get four counters in a row, either horizontally, vertically or diagonally.

10	45	16	36	56	7
27	64	80	100	48	2
70	20	54	15	81	14
8	24	72	90	63	28
50	42	60	49	32	3
1	12	40	25	35	18
6	9	21	4	30	5

A	B
1	10
2	9
3	8
4	7
5	6
6	5
7	4
8	3
9	2
10	1

You can also play on your own and see how many squares you can cover.

Children can use a calculator to check the answers. By altering the numbers involved, you can use this activity to practise a whole range of number facts: addition, subtraction or division.

TAKE ONE

Look back to page 14, then try these:

2×10=   3×20=   5×30=

As you have seen, whole sets of 10 are quite easy to multiply.

But what about:

3×19   4×29   or   6×39

At first, these look more difficult, especially if you try to do them in your head the same way as you would on paper.

2×19=   (2×20)−2=

3×19=   (3×20)−3=

4×19=   (4×20)−4=

5×19=   (5×20)−5=

Try these number patterns using a calculator and see if you notice anything.

2×29=   (2×30)−2=

3×29=   (3×30)−3=

4×29=   (4×30)−4=

5×29=   (5×30)−5=

Look back at page 18.
Did you spot that the answers in each row are the same?

This is because you can think of 19 as $(20-1)$, and 29 as $(30-1)$ and so on.

So, you can think of 3×19 as $3\times(20-1)$ which is the same as $(3\times20)-(3\times1)$ or $(3\times20)-3$.

Now try these in your head:

Think of 2×39 as $(2\times40)-2=$

3×39 as $(3\times40)-3=$

4×39 as

5×39 as

6×39 as

$2\times49=$	$2\times69=$
$3\times49=$	$3\times69=$
$4\times49=$	$4\times69=$
$7\times49=$	$8\times69=$
$9\times49=$	$6\times69=$

This activity can also be used for numbers ending in 8, e.g. you can think of 2×28 as $(2\times30)-4$; you can think of 3×28 as $(3\times30)-6$, etc.

TURNAROUND

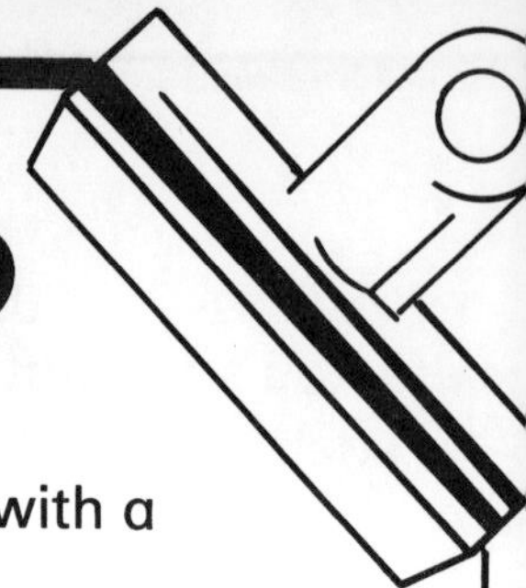

Try these pairs of calculations either in your head or with a calculator.

4+ 5=	18+ 2=	16+ 7=
5+ 4=	2+18=	7+16=
9+16=	21+12=	14+18=
16+ 9=	12+21=	18+14=

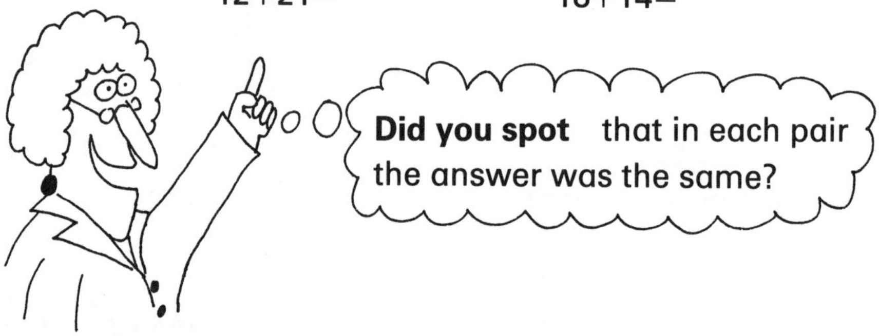

This shows you that it doesn't matter in which order we add numbers together, which can make some calculations much easier to do!

Try turning these ones round in your head before working out the answer:

e.g. 2+29 becomes 29+2 which =31

5+43=	8+31=	3+96=
7+22=	4+52=	2+77=
3+68=	6+23=	9+80=
4+61=	5+32=	2+58=

Point out to the child that you should only do this when one of the numbers to be added is much smaller than the other one.

SURPRISE SURPRISE

Follow the instructions in these flow charts for a surprise!

Flow chart 1

1. START
2. THINK OF A NUMBER
3. DOUBLE IT
4. ADD 4
5. MULTIPLY BY 3
6. SUBTRACT 12
7. DIVIDE BY 6
8. WHAT IS THE ANSWER?
9. STOP

Flow chart 2

1. START
2. THINK OF A NUMBER
3. ADD 6
4. MULTIPLY BY 2
5. SUBTRACT 12
6. SUBTRACT THE NUMBER YOU FIRST THOUGHT OF
7. WHAT IS THE ANSWER?
8. STOP

Flow chart 3

1. START
2. THINK OF TWO SINGLE DIGIT NUMBERS
3. MULTIPLY THE FIRST NUMBER BY 5
4. ADD THE SECOND NUMBER
5. MULTIPLY BY 2
6. SUBTRACT THE SECOND NUMBER
7. WHAT IS THE ANSWER?
8. STOP

Encourage the child to try several numbers with each flow chart and then, for fun and extra practice, try them out on friends. As these charts are based on the relationship between +, −, ÷ and ×, it is very useful to try to find out exactly how they work and then design some of your own.

ADD ONS

Look at these:

46	37	29
+20	+30	+40
66	67	69

As you have already seen, they are quite easy to do as only the digit in the tens column changes. But when both numbers have a units digit above 0, they become more difficult:

46	38	29
+27	+34	+46
73	72	75

Have a look at this idea as one possible way of making them easier:

46 + 27 —(+3)→ 46 + 30 = 76 —(−3)→ 73

38 —(+2)→ 40

38 + 34 → 40 + 34 = 74 —(−2)→ 72

Can you see what is happening?

You add a figure to one of the numbers so that it becomes a whole set of tens.

Then you work out the new, easier calculation, then take the same figure away from the answer.

Try this idea on the examples on the next page.

37	46	54
+19	+28	+18
___	___	___

56	48	67
+37	+25	+38
___	___	___

42	73	85
+19	+48	+18
___	___	___

65	54	48
+27	+38	+34
___	___	___

59	36	67
+23	+46	+24
___	___	___

TABLE ZIG-ZAG

Look at this grid carefully. The axis going up stands for sets of 10. The axis going across stands for the units 0 to 9. Some numbers have already been plotted on the grid. Can you see how their position was worked out?

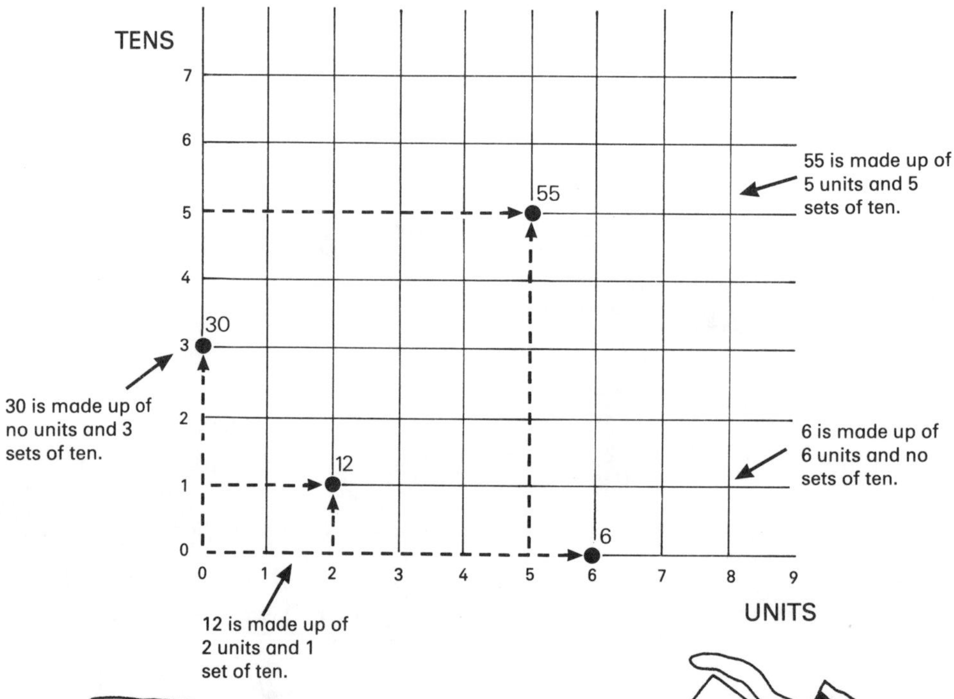

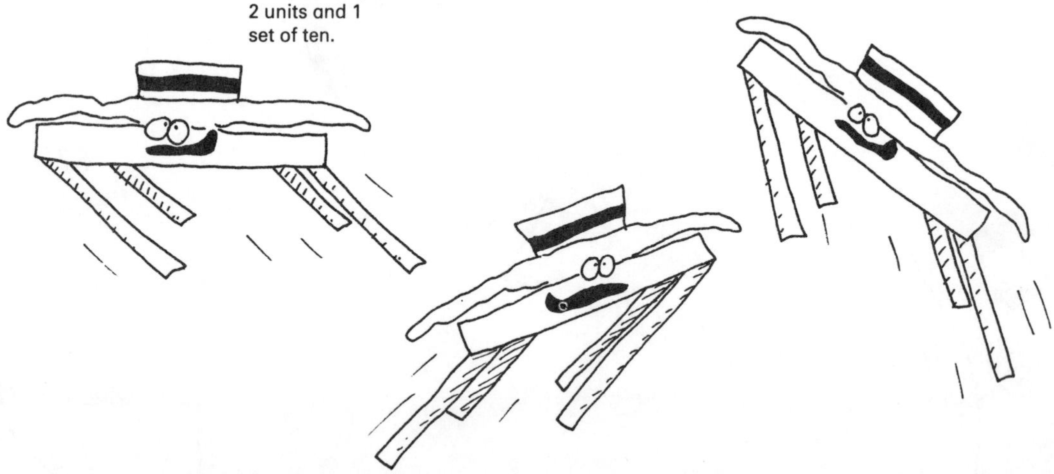

On the grid on the next page, see if you can plot the products of the 4 times table. Join up the points as you go along. The first few have been done for you.

Now, using a different colour, try plotting the products of the 6 times table.

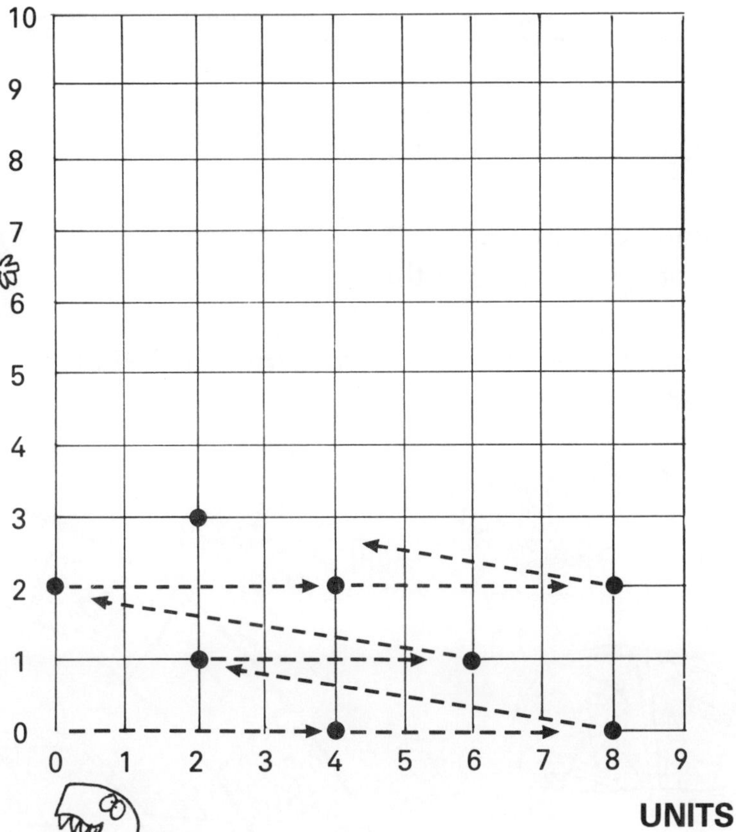

You can encourage the child to plot other tables on squared paper if she is interested. This activity practises the times tables and reinforces the idea of pattern within number.

KEEP YOUR DISTANCE

Trace and cut out the three cars. Place Angela's car with its back wheel on the start square and move it ONE square at a time up the race track. In the chart provided on the next page write down the numbers which the front wheel and rear wheel move onto each time. The first few have been done for you.

Now complete Sam's chart the same way but move him TWO sections up the track each time.

Finally, race Fred's van up the track moving THREE sections each time. Don't forget to fill in his chart!

ANGELA

FRONT WHEEL	REAR WHEEL
14	10
15	11
	12
20	16

SAM

FRONT WHEEL	REAR WHEEL
13	10
	12

FRED

FRONT WHEEL	REAR WHEEL
	10

The following examples use the numbers from these charts. What do you notice about the answers?

ANGELA	SAM	FRED
14−10=4	13−10=3	12−10=2
15−11=4	15−13=3	15−13=2
16−12=4	17−14=3	18−16=2

Did you spot that, although the numbers in each calculation change, the answers stay the same? This is because each number has changed by the same amount
e.g. in Fred's case, +3 each time.

You can use this idea to make many subtractions easy enough to do in your head.

$$\begin{array}{r} 42 \\ -37 \\ \hline \\ \hline \end{array} \xrightarrow[+3]{+3} \begin{array}{r} 45 \\ -40 \\ \hline 5 \\ \hline \end{array} \qquad \begin{array}{r} 24 \\ -18 \\ \hline \\ \hline \end{array} \xrightarrow[+2]{+2} \begin{array}{r} 26 \\ -20 \\ \hline 6 \\ \hline \end{array}$$

Make the following examples easier by increasing the number being subtracted until it is turned into a whole set of tens. But don't forget, you must add the same amount to *both* numbers!

63	24	93	56	37	25
−47	−16	−55	−48	−19	− 9
—	—	—	—	—	—
—	—	—	—	—	—

42	44	81	78	35	52
−13	−36	−53	−53	−18	−34
—	—	—	—	—	—
—	—	—	—	—	—

SPACE RACE

SPACE WARNING! Young humans should ask for help with making the spinning saucer. MESSAGE ENDS.

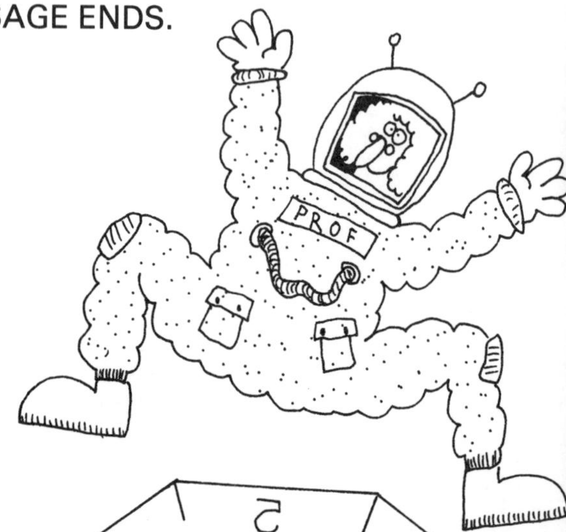

1 Trace this spinning saucer on to a piece of thick card, cut it out then colour it in.
2 Next, carefully make a hole in the middle and push through a short length of knitting needle or old ballpoint pen.
3 Finally, glue the two parts together.
4 If you have made the saucer well, it should spin for at least 20 seconds on top of a table.

Short piece of knitting needle or old ball point pen.

It is important to do the activity on the following page both mentally and with a calculator, as it should show the child that in some cases, using a calculator is less efficient than working it out in your head.

Spin the saucer slowly. When it stops, write the number it lands on in the ignition square of your rocket. Now spin the saucer hard.

Can you complete the launch sequence for each rocket and lift off before the spinning saucer comes to rest?

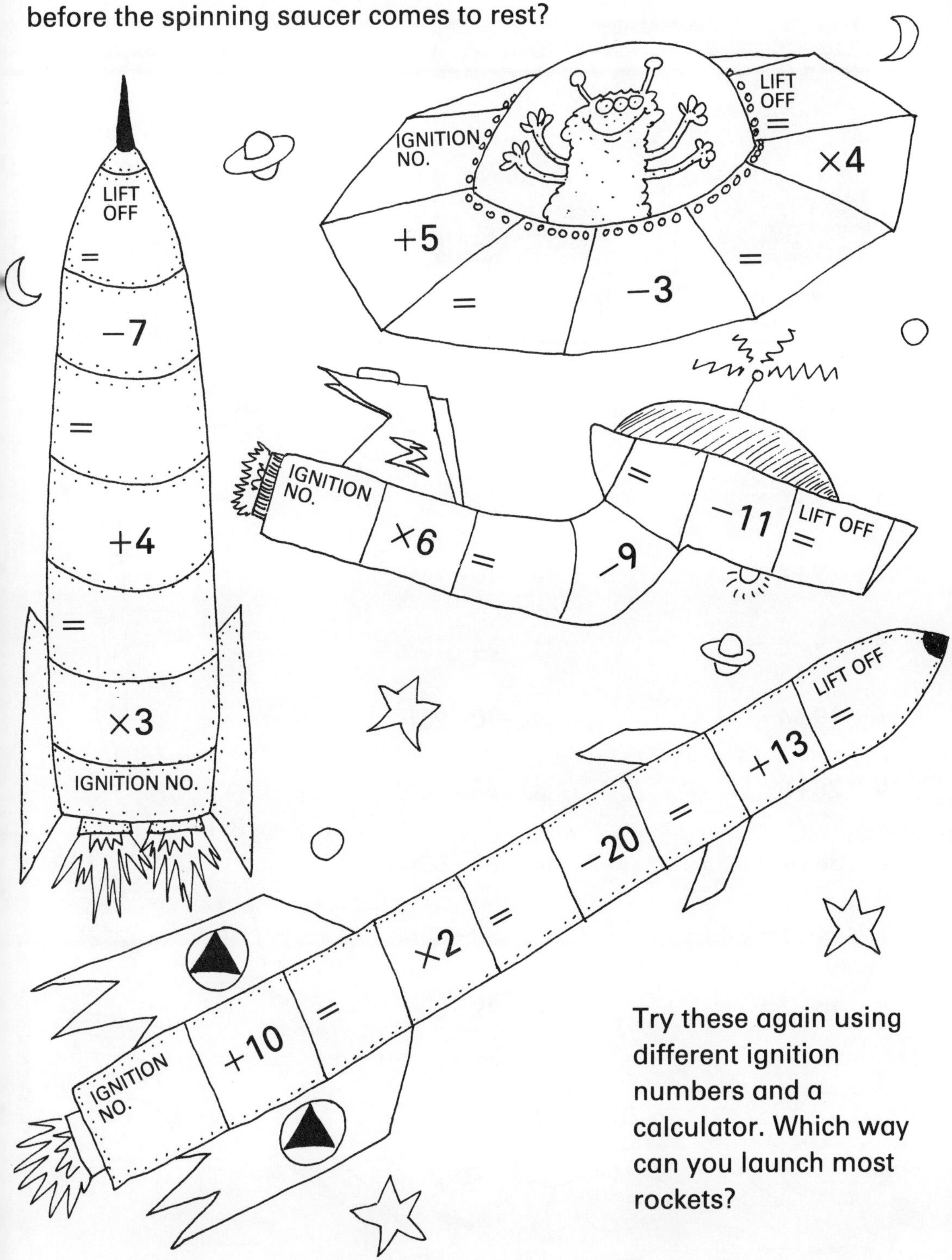

Try these again using different ignition numbers and a calculator. Which way can you launch most rockets?

CHECK-UP TIME

If you have understood and practised the ideas in this book, you should find that you can do the following examples in your head.

How many can you do in 10 minutes?

1. 8+6=
2. 9+4=
3. 9+6=
4. 19+4=
5. 26+6=
6. 38+7=
7. 24−9=
8. 46−7=
9. 23− 5=
10. 16+10=
11. 34+10=
12. 70+20=
13. 45−10=
14. 82−50=
15. 53−30=
16. 79−60=

17. $9 \times 10 =$

18. $8 \times 10 =$

19. $11 \times 10 =$

20. $3 \times 49 =$

21. $4 \times 69 =$

22. $5 \times 29 =$

23. $3 + 25 =$

24. $6 + 17 =$

25. $46 + 28 =$

26. $36 + 18 =$

27. $75 + 27 =$

28. $62 - 46 =$

29. $55 - 47 =$

30. $35 - 28 =$

It is most important that tests of any kind take place in an atmosphere of *trust and encouragement*. Never use the results to criticize the child or her school. The aim here is to identify what she has and has not learned or understood. You should then try to use this information positively to give extra practice or explanation as appropriate. To help you, the examples on these pages relate to the activities as follows:

p4: 1–3	**p13: 13–16**	**p20: 22–23**
p5: 4–6	**p14 & 15: 17–19**	**p22 & 23: 24–26**
p10: 7–9	**p18 & 19: 20–21**	**p26 & 27: 27–30**

GLOSSARY

Many primary schools now introduce children to the correct mathematical terms associated with each concept. This allows children to talk accurately about the work they do, which in turn helps them to understand it better.

As some of these terms may be unfamiliar to parents, a glossary of those used in this book is provided here.

DIGITS AND NUMBERS
Our number system comprises the DIGITS 1 to 9 together with the placeholder 0. A NUMBER is made up of one or more DIGITS, e.g. the NUMBER 23 comprises the DIGITS 2 and 3.

FACE
A geometric plane making up a solid, e.g. a cube has six FACES, each one a square.

NET
A diagram which, when cut from paper or card, folds up into a SOLID.

NUMBER BONDS
Numbers which are linked together in a mathematical statement, e.g. number bonds to 20 would include: 1+19; 2+18; 3+17 or 20−5=15; 20−7=13, etc. Multiplication tables are another example.

PLACE VALUE
In our number system the value of any digit is determined by its position or place, e.g. in 122, the 2 in the tens column has a value of 20, which is ten times greater than the value of the 2 in the units column. This is one of the most difficult ideas for young children to grasp.

PLANE SHAPE
A two-dimensional shape.

PRODUCT
The answer to a multiplication, e.g. 60 is the product of 12 and 5.

SET
A collection of objects, letters or numbers which are distinguishable from each other.

SOLID
A three-dimensional shape.

SUM
The answer to an addition, e.g. 23 is the SUM of 14 and 9.